MW00784288
EXCEL
STILL
MORE

Published by
Spiritbuilding Publishers
9700 Ferry Road, Waynesville, OH 45068
(800) 282-4901

ESM Journal
by Kris Emerson

ISBN: 9781964805078

Spiritbuilding
PUBLISHERS
spiritbuilding.com

Welcome to the ESM Journal!

Thank you for joining us on this mission to get better every single day. This journal is a companion to the "Excel Still More" podcast and is designed to give you things to read, write, consider and pray to build daily confidence and direction. Also, there is a weekly section so you can document your imporvement in faith, fitness, finance and friendships. Please note the sample pages and the podcast episodes below that assist with many of these elements.

Episode 2: One Great Hour

Episode 8: Four Fold Excellence

Episode 9: Asking Beautiful Questions

Episode 11: Eat the Frog

Episode 14: Motion is Lotion

Episode 17: Your Daily Highlight

Episode 19: Level Three Gratitude

Episode 21: Affirmations are Cool

May God bless you in your journey to Excel Still More!

www.ExcelStillMore.life

Excel Still More **excel.still.more** **@KrisEmersonESM**

4-FOLD EXCELLENCE (ESM Ep. 8) *Weekly Progress*

A great way to track progress is to excel in four key areas every week. If each week includes signs of measurable efforts in faith building, financial wisdom, friendship development, and fitness choices, this will add up to amazing progress! So as your week goes by, keep referencing back to this section to note specific things you did to grow in these areas.

FAITH

Examples:
Monday - I listened to a sermon online about Gossip.

Thursday - I just sat and prayed for 20 minutes. Longest in a year

Saturday - My family and I sat down and did our Bible class lessons together.

FINANCES

Examples:
Tuesday - I did NOT buy anything from Amazon!

Wednesday - I paid a little extra on the credit card bill.

Friday - We ate at home instead of going out, saving like $50!

Date/Week: 5/5 - 5/11, Week 1

Remember: Excellence develops in these areas when you...
1. Care about getting better.
2. Have a clear direction of what better looks like.
3. Get an education as to new ideas to pursue.
4. Embrace the discipline that will be needed.
5. Find a community of supporters who share your goals.

FRIENDSHIP

Examples:
Tuesday - I sent a text to an old friend who has been going through a tough time.

Friday - We asked a family over for dinner tonight and had a great time.

Sunday - I spent time after church chatting with a new church member.

FITNESS

Examples:
Monday - The family and I went to a local park and played for a half hour.

Thursday - I got out for a 30-minutes walk this evening

Saturday - I shot some hoops and just tried to stay outside most of today.

Date/Day: 5/6/19, Monday

YESTERDAY: This space is for interesting and memorable events that you remember from yesterday. These are things that happened after you closed the journal and had some effect on you. This is a great place to detail a Surprise Daily Highlight: something impactful and powerful that you didn't expect (an event, conversation, or realization).

ASK BEAUTIFUL QUESTIONS: (ESM Ep. 9) A simple approach to this section is to make a list of prayer requests. You can list people who need God's help, circumstances where you need God, and things that are heavy on your heart. Another approach is to actually ask big questions: "God, will you heal..." "Father, can you take control of..." "Lord, what am I missing with regard to..." Just be open and honest with God about your needs.

BIBLE READ and NOTES: Write in the book and chapter(s) you will be reading today. Then, document things you learned from the text. What is God showing you? What are practical things you plan to do with the lessons learned in this text? Be open and honest about the effect the Word is having on you.

Suggestion: read one chapter per day. Look for Jesus in that chapter. Write things about Him, about who He is or what He does. Then note some things you plan to do with that today.

TODAY'S SCHEDULE: This is the place for some basic daily planning. What are the things you need to do today? Write in events, people, and associated times, to get a snapshot of today's schedule. Note: if you are married, this is a good time to ask them what "we" have planned today.

EAT THAT FROG: (ESM Ep. 11) Write down one thing, maybe two, that is important to get done today, even though you don't want to do it. Knock this out as early in the day as you can!

MY DAILY HIGHLIGHT: (ESM Ep. 17) Alright, now write down one thing, maybe two, that is important and you are excited about doing it. This will make today a great day! Make sure to get this done today!

LEVEL 3 GRATITUDE: (ESM Ep. 19) Note things you are thankful for. But also, attribute all glory to God. Finally, tell God what you will do out of gratitude today. Example: "Thank you for my family. You have blessed this home greatly. We will sit down tonight and read your Word together."

AFFIRMATIONS ARE COOL: (ESM Ep. 21) Lastly, write down some things about yourself, about your determination, ability, focus and faith. You can attach God to this, since He your strength. Similar to "I can do all things through Christ who strengthens me," what do you plan to do today or be, in the name of Jesus Christ? Be definite. Be bold. Affirm.

A great way to track progress is to excel in four key areas every week. If each week includes signs of measurable efforts in faith building, financial wisdom, friendship development, and fitness choices, this will add up to amazing progress! So as your week goes by, keep referencing back to this section to note specific things you did to grow in these areas.

FAITH

FINANCES

Remember: Excellence develops in these areas when you...
1. Care about getting better.
2. Have a clear direction of what better looks like.
3. Get an education as to new ideas to pursue.
4. Embrace the discipline that will be needed.
5. Find a community of supporters who share your goals.

FRIENDSHIP

FITNESS

Date/Day:

YESTERDAY:

ASK BEAUTIFUL QUESTIONS:

BIBLE READ and NOTES:

TODAY'S SCHEDULE:

EAT THAT FROG:

MY DAILY HIGHLIGHT:

LEVEL 3 GRATITUDE:

AFFIRMATIONS ARE COOL:

Date/Day:

YESTERDAY:

ASK BEAUTIFUL QUESTIONS:

BIBLE READ and NOTES:

TODAY'S SCHEDULE:

EAT THAT FROG:

MY DAILY HIGHLIGHT:

LEVEL 3 GRATITUDE:

AFFIRMATIONS ARE COOL:

Date/Day:

YESTERDAY:

ASK BEAUTIFUL QUESTIONS:

BIBLE READ and NOTES:

TODAY'S SCHEDULE:

EAT THAT FROG:

MY DAILY HIGHLIGHT:

LEVEL 3 GRATITUDE:

AFFIRMATIONS ARE COOL:

Date/Day:

YESTERDAY:

ASK BEAUTIFUL QUESTIONS:

BIBLE READ and NOTES:

TODAY'S SCHEDULE:

EAT THAT FROG:

MY DAILY HIGHLIGHT:

LEVEL 3 GRATITUDE:

AFFIRMATIONS ARE COOL:

Date/Day:

YESTERDAY:

ASK BEAUTIFUL QUESTIONS:

BIBLE READ and NOTES:

TODAY'S SCHEDULE:

EAT THAT FROG:

MY DAILY HIGHLIGHT:

LEVEL 3 GRATITUDE:

AFFIRMATIONS ARE COOL:

Date/Day:

YESTERDAY:

ASK BEAUTIFUL QUESTIONS:

BIBLE READ and NOTES:

TODAY'S SCHEDULE:

EAT THAT FROG:

MY DAILY HIGHLIGHT:

LEVEL 3 GRATITUDE:

AFFIRMATIONS ARE COOL:

Date/Day:

YESTERDAY:

ASK BEAUTIFUL QUESTIONS:

BIBLE READ and NOTES:

TODAY'S SCHEDULE:

EAT THAT FROG:

MY DAILY HIGHLIGHT:

LEVEL 3 GRATITUDE:

AFFIRMATIONS ARE COOL:

A great way to track progress is to excel in four key areas every week. If each week includes signs of measurable efforts in faith building, financial wisdom, friendship development, and fitness choices, this will add up to amazing progress! So as your week goes by, keep referencing back to this section to note specific things you did to grow in these areas.

FAITH

FINANCES

Remember: Excellence develops in these areas when you...
1. *Care about getting better.*
2. *Have a clear direction of what better looks like.*
3. *Get an education as to new ideas to pursue.*
4. *Embrace the discipline that will be needed.*
5. *Find a community of supporters who share your goals.*

FRIENDSHIP

FITNESS

Date/Day:

YESTERDAY:

ASK BEAUTIFUL QUESTIONS:

BIBLE READ and NOTES:

TODAY'S SCHEDULE:

EAT THAT FROG:

MY DAILY HIGHLIGHT:

LEVEL 3 GRATITUDE:

AFFIRMATIONS ARE COOL:

Date/Day:

YESTERDAY:

ASK BEAUTIFUL QUESTIONS:

BIBLE READ and NOTES:

TODAY'S SCHEDULE:

EAT THAT FROG:

MY DAILY HIGHLIGHT:

LEVEL 3 GRATITUDE:

AFFIRMATIONS ARE COOL:

Date/Day:

YESTERDAY:

ASK BEAUTIFUL QUESTIONS:

BIBLE READ and NOTES:

TODAY'S SCHEDULE:

EAT THAT FROG:

MY DAILY HIGHLIGHT:

LEVEL 3 GRATITUDE:

AFFIRMATIONS ARE COOL:

Date/Day:

YESTERDAY:

ASK BEAUTIFUL QUESTIONS:

BIBLE READ and NOTES:

TODAY'S SCHEDULE:

EAT THAT FROG:

MY DAILY HIGHLIGHT:

LEVEL 3 GRATITUDE:

AFFIRMATIONS ARE COOL:

Date/Day:

YESTERDAY:

ASK BEAUTIFUL QUESTIONS:

BIBLE READ and NOTES:

TODAY'S SCHEDULE:

EAT THAT FROG:

MY DAILY HIGHLIGHT:

LEVEL 3 GRATITUDE:

AFFIRMATIONS ARE COOL:

Date/Day:

YESTERDAY:

ASK BEAUTIFUL QUESTIONS:

BIBLE READ and NOTES:

TODAY'S SCHEDULE:

EAT THAT FROG:

MY DAILY HIGHLIGHT:

LEVEL 3 GRATITUDE:

AFFIRMATIONS ARE COOL:

Date/Day:

YESTERDAY:

ASK BEAUTIFUL QUESTIONS:

BIBLE READ and NOTES:

TODAY'S SCHEDULE:

EAT THAT FROG:

MY DAILY HIGHLIGHT:

LEVEL 3 GRATITUDE:

AFFIRMATIONS ARE COOL:

A great way to track progress is to excel in four key areas every week. If each week includes signs of measurable efforts in faith building, financial wisdom, friendship development, and fitness choices, this will add up to amazing progress! So as your week goes by, keep referencing back to this section to note specific things you did to grow in these areas.

FAITH

FINANCES

Remember: Excellence develops in these areas when you...
1. Care about getting better.
2. Have a clear direction of what better looks like.
3. Get an education as to new ideas to pursue.
4. Embrace the discipline that will be needed.
5. Find a community of supporters who share your goals.

FRIENDSHIP

FITNESS

Date/Day:

YESTERDAY:

ASK BEAUTIFUL QUESTIONS:

BIBLE READ and NOTES:

TODAY'S SCHEDULE:

EAT THAT FROG:

MY DAILY HIGHLIGHT:

LEVEL 3 GRATITUDE:

AFFIRMATIONS ARE COOL:

Date/Day:

YESTERDAY:

ASK BEAUTIFUL QUESTIONS:

BIBLE READ and NOTES:

TODAY'S SCHEDULE:

EAT THAT FROG:

MY DAILY HIGHLIGHT:

LEVEL 3 GRATITUDE:

AFFIRMATIONS ARE COOL:

Date/Day:

YESTERDAY:

ASK BEAUTIFUL QUESTIONS:

BIBLE READ and NOTES:

TODAY'S SCHEDULE:

EAT THAT FROG:

MY DAILY HIGHLIGHT:

LEVEL 3 GRATITUDE:

AFFIRMATIONS ARE COOL:

Date/Day:

YESTERDAY:

ASK BEAUTIFUL QUESTIONS:

BIBLE READ and NOTES:

TODAY'S SCHEDULE:

EAT THAT FROG:

MY DAILY HIGHLIGHT:

LEVEL 3 GRATITUDE:

AFFIRMATIONS ARE COOL:

Date/Day:

YESTERDAY:

ASK BEAUTIFUL QUESTIONS:

BIBLE READ and NOTES:

TODAY'S SCHEDULE:

EAT THAT FROG:

MY DAILY HIGHLIGHT:

LEVEL 3 GRATITUDE:

AFFIRMATIONS ARE COOL:

Date/Day:

YESTERDAY:

ASK BEAUTIFUL QUESTIONS:

BIBLE READ and NOTES:

TODAY'S SCHEDULE:

EAT THAT FROG:

MY DAILY HIGHLIGHT:

LEVEL 3 GRATITUDE:

AFFIRMATIONS ARE COOL:

Date/Day:

YESTERDAY:

ASK BEAUTIFUL QUESTIONS:

BIBLE READ and NOTES:

TODAY'S SCHEDULE:

EAT THAT FROG:

MY DAILY HIGHLIGHT:

LEVEL 3 GRATITUDE:

AFFIRMATIONS ARE COOL:

4-FOLD EXCELLENCE

A great way to track progress is to excel in four key areas every week. If each week includes signs of measurable efforts in faith building, financial wisdom, friendship development, and fitness choices, this will add up to amazing progress! So as your week goes by, keep referencing back to this section to note specific things you did to grow in these areas.

FAITH

FINANCES

Remember: Excellence develops in these areas when you...
1. Care about getting better.
2. Have a clear direction of what better looks like.
3. Get an education as to new ideas to pursue.
4. Embrace the discipline that will be needed.
5. Find a community of supporters who share your goals.

FRIENDSHIP

FITNESS

Date/Day:

YESTERDAY:

ASK BEAUTIFUL QUESTIONS:

BIBLE READ and NOTES:

TODAY'S SCHEDULE:

EAT THAT FROG:

MY DAILY HIGHLIGHT:

LEVEL 3 GRATITUDE:

AFFIRMATIONS ARE COOL:

Date/Day:

YESTERDAY:

ASK BEAUTIFUL QUESTIONS:

BIBLE READ and NOTES:

TODAY'S SCHEDULE:

EAT THAT FROG:

MY DAILY HIGHLIGHT:

LEVEL 3 GRATITUDE:

AFFIRMATIONS ARE COOL:

Date/Day:

YESTERDAY:

ASK BEAUTIFUL QUESTIONS:

BIBLE READ and NOTES:

TODAY'S SCHEDULE:

EAT THAT FROG:

MY DAILY HIGHLIGHT:

LEVEL 3 GRATITUDE:

AFFIRMATIONS ARE COOL:

Date/Day:

YESTERDAY:

ASK BEAUTIFUL QUESTIONS:

BIBLE READ and NOTES:

TODAY'S SCHEDULE:

EAT THAT FROG:

MY DAILY HIGHLIGHT:

LEVEL 3 GRATITUDE:

AFFIRMATIONS ARE COOL:

Date/Day:

YESTERDAY:

ASK BEAUTIFUL QUESTIONS:

BIBLE READ and NOTES:

TODAY'S SCHEDULE:

EAT THAT FROG:

MY DAILY HIGHLIGHT:

LEVEL 3 GRATITUDE:

AFFIRMATIONS ARE COOL:

Date/Day:

YESTERDAY:

ASK BEAUTIFUL QUESTIONS:

BIBLE READ and NOTES:

TODAY'S SCHEDULE:

EAT THAT FROG:

MY DAILY HIGHLIGHT:

LEVEL 3 GRATITUDE:

AFFIRMATIONS ARE COOL:

Date/Day:

YESTERDAY:

ASK BEAUTIFUL QUESTIONS:

BIBLE READ and NOTES:

TODAY'S SCHEDULE:

EAT THAT FROG:

MY DAILY HIGHLIGHT:

LEVEL 3 GRATITUDE:

AFFIRMATIONS ARE COOL:

4-FOLD EXCELLENCE

A great way to track progress is to excel in four key areas every week. If each week includes signs of measurable efforts in faith building, financial wisdom, friendship development, and fitness choices, this will add up to amazing progress! So as your week goes by, keep referencing back to this section to note specific things you did to grow in these areas.

FAITH

FINANCES

Remember: Excellence develops in these areas when you...
1. Care about getting better.
2. Have a clear direction of what better looks like.
3. Get an education as to new ideas to pursue.
4. Embrace the discipline that will be needed.
5. Find a community of supporters who share your goals.

FRIENDSHIP

FITNESS

Date/Day:

YESTERDAY:

ASK BEAUTIFUL QUESTIONS:

BIBLE READ and NOTES:

TODAY'S SCHEDULE:

EAT THAT FROG:

MY DAILY HIGHLIGHT:

LEVEL 3 GRATITUDE:

AFFIRMATIONS ARE COOL:

Date/Day:

YESTERDAY:

ASK BEAUTIFUL QUESTIONS:

BIBLE READ and NOTES:

TODAY'S SCHEDULE:

EAT THAT FROG:

MY DAILY HIGHLIGHT:

LEVEL 3 GRATITUDE:

AFFIRMATIONS ARE COOL:

Date/Day:

YESTERDAY:

ASK BEAUTIFUL QUESTIONS:

BIBLE READ and NOTES:

TODAY'S SCHEDULE:

EAT THAT FROG:

MY DAILY HIGHLIGHT:

LEVEL 3 GRATITUDE:

AFFIRMATIONS ARE COOL:

Date/Day:

YESTERDAY:

ASK BEAUTIFUL QUESTIONS:

BIBLE READ and NOTES:

TODAY'S SCHEDULE:

EAT THAT FROG:

MY DAILY HIGHLIGHT:

LEVEL 3 GRATITUDE:

AFFIRMATIONS ARE COOL:

Date/Day:

YESTERDAY:

ASK BEAUTIFUL QUESTIONS:

BIBLE READ and NOTES:

TODAY'S SCHEDULE:

EAT THAT FROG:

MY DAILY HIGHLIGHT:

LEVEL 3 GRATITUDE:

AFFIRMATIONS ARE COOL:

Date/Day:

YESTERDAY:

ASK BEAUTIFUL QUESTIONS:

BIBLE READ and NOTES:

TODAY'S SCHEDULE:

EAT THAT FROG:

MY DAILY HIGHLIGHT:

LEVEL 3 GRATITUDE:

AFFIRMATIONS ARE COOL:

Date/Day:

YESTERDAY:

ASK BEAUTIFUL QUESTIONS:

BIBLE READ and NOTES:

TODAY'S SCHEDULE:

EAT THAT FROG:

MY DAILY HIGHLIGHT:

LEVEL 3 GRATITUDE:

AFFIRMATIONS ARE COOL:

A great way to track progress is to excel in four key areas every week. If each week includes signs of measurable efforts in faith building, financial wisdom, friendship development, and fitness choices, this will add up to amazing progress! So as your week goes by, keep referencing back to this section to note specific things you did to grow in these areas.

FAITH

FINANCES

Remember: Excellence develops in these areas when you...
1. Care about getting better.
2. Have a clear direction of what better looks like.
3. Get an education as to new ideas to pursue.
4. Embrace the discipline that will be needed.
5. Find a community of supporters who share your goals.

FRIENDSHIP

FITNESS

Date/Day:

YESTERDAY:

ASK BEAUTIFUL QUESTIONS:

BIBLE READ and NOTES:

TODAY'S SCHEDULE:

EAT THAT FROG:

MY DAILY HIGHLIGHT:

LEVEL 3 GRATITUDE:

AFFIRMATIONS ARE COOL:

Date/Day:

YESTERDAY:

ASK BEAUTIFUL QUESTIONS:

BIBLE READ and NOTES:

TODAY'S SCHEDULE:

EAT THAT FROG:

MY DAILY HIGHLIGHT:

LEVEL 3 GRATITUDE:

AFFIRMATIONS ARE COOL:

Date/Day:

YESTERDAY:

ASK BEAUTIFUL QUESTIONS:

BIBLE READ and NOTES:

TODAY'S SCHEDULE:

EAT THAT FROG:

MY DAILY HIGHLIGHT:

LEVEL 3 GRATITUDE:

AFFIRMATIONS ARE COOL:

Date/Day:

YESTERDAY:

ASK BEAUTIFUL QUESTIONS:

BIBLE READ and NOTES:

TODAY'S SCHEDULE:

EAT THAT FROG:

MY DAILY HIGHLIGHT:

LEVEL 3 GRATITUDE:

AFFIRMATIONS ARE COOL:

Date/Day:

YESTERDAY:

ASK BEAUTIFUL QUESTIONS:

BIBLE READ and NOTES:

TODAY'S SCHEDULE:

EAT THAT FROG:

MY DAILY HIGHLIGHT:

LEVEL 3 GRATITUDE:

AFFIRMATIONS ARE COOL:

Date/Day:

YESTERDAY:

ASK BEAUTIFUL QUESTIONS:

BIBLE READ and NOTES:

TODAY'S SCHEDULE:

EAT THAT FROG:

MY DAILY HIGHLIGHT:

LEVEL 3 GRATITUDE:

AFFIRMATIONS ARE COOL:

Date/Day:

YESTERDAY:

ASK BEAUTIFUL QUESTIONS:

BIBLE READ and NOTES:

TODAY'S SCHEDULE:

EAT THAT FROG:

MY DAILY HIGHLIGHT:

LEVEL 3 GRATITUDE:

AFFIRMATIONS ARE COOL:

4-FOLD EXCELLENCE

A great way to track progress is to excel in four key areas every week. If each week includes signs of measurable efforts in faith building, financial wisdom, friendship development, and fitness choices, this will add up to amazing progress! So as your week goes by, keep referencing back to this section to note specific things you did to grow in these areas.

FAITH

FINANCES

Date/Week:

Remember: Excellence develops in these areas when you...
1. Care about getting better.
2. Have a clear direction of what better looks like.
3. Get an education as to new ideas to pursue.
4. Embrace the discipline that will be needed.
5. Find a community of supporters who share your goals.

FRIENDSHIP

FITNESS

Date/Day:

YESTERDAY:

ASK BEAUTIFUL QUESTIONS:

BIBLE READ and NOTES:

TODAY'S SCHEDULE:

EAT THAT FROG:

MY DAILY HIGHLIGHT:

LEVEL 3 GRATITUDE:

AFFIRMATIONS ARE COOL:

Date/Day:

YESTERDAY:

ASK BEAUTIFUL QUESTIONS:

BIBLE READ and NOTES:

TODAY'S SCHEDULE:

EAT THAT FROG:

MY DAILY HIGHLIGHT:

LEVEL 3 GRATITUDE:

AFFIRMATIONS ARE COOL:

Date/Day:

YESTERDAY:

ASK BEAUTIFUL QUESTIONS:

BIBLE READ and NOTES:

TODAY'S SCHEDULE:

EAT THAT FROG:

MY DAILY HIGHLIGHT:

LEVEL 3 GRATITUDE:

AFFIRMATIONS ARE COOL:

Date/Day:

YESTERDAY:

ASK BEAUTIFUL QUESTIONS:

BIBLE READ and NOTES:

TODAY'S SCHEDULE:

EAT THAT FROG:

MY DAILY HIGHLIGHT:

LEVEL 3 GRATITUDE:

AFFIRMATIONS ARE COOL:

Date/Day:

YESTERDAY:

ASK BEAUTIFUL QUESTIONS:

BIBLE READ and NOTES:

TODAY'S SCHEDULE:

EAT THAT FROG:

MY DAILY HIGHLIGHT:

LEVEL 3 GRATITUDE:

AFFIRMATIONS ARE COOL:

Date/Day:

YESTERDAY:

ASK BEAUTIFUL QUESTIONS:

BIBLE READ and NOTES:

TODAY'S SCHEDULE:

EAT THAT FROG:

MY DAILY HIGHLIGHT:

LEVEL 3 GRATITUDE:

AFFIRMATIONS ARE COOL:

Date/Day:

YESTERDAY:

ASK BEAUTIFUL QUESTIONS:

BIBLE READ and NOTES:

TODAY'S SCHEDULE:

EAT THAT FROG:

MY DAILY HIGHLIGHT:

LEVEL 3 GRATITUDE:

AFFIRMATIONS ARE COOL:

A great way to track progress is to excel in four key areas every week. If each week includes signs of measurable efforts in faith building, financial wisdom, friendship development, and fitness choices, this will add up to amazing progress! So as your week goes by, keep referencing back to this section to note specific things you did to grow in these areas.

FAITH

FINANCES

Remember: Excellence develops in these areas when you...
1. Care about getting better.
2. Have a clear direction of what better looks like.
3. Get an education as to new ideas to pursue.
4. Embrace the discipline that will be needed.
5. Find a community of supporters who share your goals.

FRIENDSHIP

FITNESS

Date/Day:

YESTERDAY:

ASK BEAUTIFUL QUESTIONS:

BIBLE READ and NOTES:

TODAY'S SCHEDULE:

EAT THAT FROG:

MY DAILY HIGHLIGHT:

LEVEL 3 GRATITUDE:

AFFIRMATIONS ARE COOL:

Date/Day:

YESTERDAY:

ASK BEAUTIFUL QUESTIONS:

BIBLE READ and NOTES:

TODAY'S SCHEDULE:

EAT THAT FROG:

MY DAILY HIGHLIGHT:

LEVEL 3 GRATITUDE:

AFFIRMATIONS ARE COOL:

Date/Day:

YESTERDAY:

ASK BEAUTIFUL QUESTIONS:

BIBLE READ and NOTES:

TODAY'S SCHEDULE:

EAT THAT FROG:

MY DAILY HIGHLIGHT:

LEVEL 3 GRATITUDE:

AFFIRMATIONS ARE COOL:

Date/Day:

YESTERDAY:

ASK BEAUTIFUL QUESTIONS:

BIBLE READ and NOTES:

TODAY'S SCHEDULE:

EAT THAT FROG:

MY DAILY HIGHLIGHT:

LEVEL 3 GRATITUDE:

AFFIRMATIONS ARE COOL:

Date/Day:

YESTERDAY:

ASK BEAUTIFUL QUESTIONS:

BIBLE READ and NOTES:

TODAY'S SCHEDULE:

EAT THAT FROG:

MY DAILY HIGHLIGHT:

LEVEL 3 GRATITUDE:

AFFIRMATIONS ARE COOL:

Date/Day:

YESTERDAY:

ASK BEAUTIFUL QUESTIONS:

BIBLE READ and NOTES:

TODAY'S SCHEDULE:

EAT THAT FROG:

MY DAILY HIGHLIGHT:

LEVEL 3 GRATITUDE:

AFFIRMATIONS ARE COOL:

Date/Day:

YESTERDAY:

ASK BEAUTIFUL QUESTIONS:

BIBLE READ and NOTES:

TODAY'S SCHEDULE:

EAT THAT FROG:

MY DAILY HIGHLIGHT:

LEVEL 3 GRATITUDE:

AFFIRMATIONS ARE COOL:

4-FOLD EXCELLENCE

A great way to track progress is to excel in four key areas every week. If each week includes signs of measurable efforts in faith building, financial wisdom, friendship development, and fitness choices, this will add up to amazing progress! So as your week goes by, keep referencing back to this section to note specific things you did to grow in these areas.

FAITH

FINANCES

Remember: Excellence develops in these areas when you...
1. Care about getting better.
2. Have a clear direction of what better looks like.
3. Get an education as to new ideas to pursue.
4. Embrace the discipline that will be needed.
5. Find a community of supporters who share your goals.

FRIENDSHIP

FITNESS

Date/Day:

YESTERDAY:

ASK BEAUTIFUL QUESTIONS:

BIBLE READ and NOTES:

TODAY'S SCHEDULE:

EAT THAT FROG:

MY DAILY HIGHLIGHT:

LEVEL 3 GRATITUDE:

AFFIRMATIONS ARE COOL:

Date/Day:

YESTERDAY:

ASK BEAUTIFUL QUESTIONS:

BIBLE READ and NOTES:

TODAY'S SCHEDULE:

EAT THAT FROG:

MY DAILY HIGHLIGHT:

LEVEL 3 GRATITUDE:

AFFIRMATIONS ARE COOL:

Date/Day:

YESTERDAY:

ASK BEAUTIFUL QUESTIONS:

BIBLE READ and NOTES:

TODAY'S SCHEDULE:

EAT THAT FROG:

MY DAILY HIGHLIGHT:

LEVEL 3 GRATITUDE:

AFFIRMATIONS ARE COOL:

Date/Day:

YESTERDAY:

ASK BEAUTIFUL QUESTIONS:

BIBLE READ and NOTES:

TODAY'S SCHEDULE:

EAT THAT FROG:

MY DAILY HIGHLIGHT:

LEVEL 3 GRATITUDE:

AFFIRMATIONS ARE COOL:

Date/Day:

YESTERDAY:

ASK BEAUTIFUL QUESTIONS:

BIBLE READ and NOTES:

TODAY'S SCHEDULE:

EAT THAT FROG:

MY DAILY HIGHLIGHT:

LEVEL 3 GRATITUDE:

AFFIRMATIONS ARE COOL:

Date/Day:

YESTERDAY:

ASK BEAUTIFUL QUESTIONS:

BIBLE READ and NOTES:

TODAY'S SCHEDULE:

EAT THAT FROG:

MY DAILY HIGHLIGHT:

LEVEL 3 GRATITUDE:

AFFIRMATIONS ARE COOL:

Date/Day:

YESTERDAY:

ASK BEAUTIFUL QUESTIONS:

BIBLE READ and NOTES:

TODAY'S SCHEDULE:

EAT THAT FROG:

MY DAILY HIGHLIGHT:

LEVEL 3 GRATITUDE:

AFFIRMATIONS ARE COOL:

4-FOLD EXCELLENCE

Weekly Progress

A great way to track progress is to excel in four key areas every week. If each week includes signs of measurable efforts in faith building, financial wisdom, friendship development, and fitness choices, this will add up to amazing progress! So as your week goes by, keep referencing back to this section to note specific things you did to grow in these areas.

FAITH

FINANCES

Date/Week:

Remember: Excellence develops in these areas when you...
1. Care about getting better.
2. Have a clear direction of what better looks like.
3. Get an education as to new ideas to pursue.
4. Embrace the discipline that will be needed.
5. Find a community of supporters who share your goals.

FRIENDSHIP

FITNESS

Date/Day:

YESTERDAY:

ASK BEAUTIFUL QUESTIONS:

BIBLE READ and NOTES:

TODAY'S SCHEDULE:

EAT THAT FROG:

MY DAILY HIGHLIGHT:

LEVEL 3 GRATITUDE:

AFFIRMATIONS ARE COOL:

Date/Day:

YESTERDAY:

ASK BEAUTIFUL QUESTIONS:

BIBLE READ and NOTES:

TODAY'S SCHEDULE:

EAT THAT FROG:

MY DAILY HIGHLIGHT:

LEVEL 3 GRATITUDE:

AFFIRMATIONS ARE COOL:

Date/Day:

YESTERDAY:

ASK BEAUTIFUL QUESTIONS:

BIBLE READ and NOTES:

TODAY'S SCHEDULE:

EAT THAT FROG:

MY DAILY HIGHLIGHT:

LEVEL 3 GRATITUDE:

AFFIRMATIONS ARE COOL:

Date/Day:

YESTERDAY:

ASK BEAUTIFUL QUESTIONS:

BIBLE READ and NOTES:

TODAY'S SCHEDULE:

EAT THAT FROG:

MY DAILY HIGHLIGHT:

LEVEL 3 GRATITUDE:

AFFIRMATIONS ARE COOL:

Date/Day:

YESTERDAY:

ASK BEAUTIFUL QUESTIONS:

BIBLE READ and NOTES:

TODAY'S SCHEDULE:

EAT THAT FROG:

MY DAILY HIGHLIGHT:

LEVEL 3 GRATITUDE:

AFFIRMATIONS ARE COOL:

Date/Day:

YESTERDAY:

ASK BEAUTIFUL QUESTIONS:

BIBLE READ and NOTES:

TODAY'S SCHEDULE:

EAT THAT FROG:

MY DAILY HIGHLIGHT:

LEVEL 3 GRATITUDE:

AFFIRMATIONS ARE COOL:

Date/Day:

YESTERDAY:

ASK BEAUTIFUL QUESTIONS:

BIBLE READ and NOTES:

TODAY'S SCHEDULE:

EAT THAT FROG:

MY DAILY HIGHLIGHT:

LEVEL 3 GRATITUDE:

AFFIRMATIONS ARE COOL:

4-FOLD EXCELLENCE

A great way to track progress is to excel in four key areas every week. If each week includes signs of measurable efforts in faith building, financial wisdom, friendship development, and fitness choices, this will add up to amazing progress! So as your week goes by, keep referencing back to this section to note specific things you did to grow in these areas.

FAITH

FINANCES

Remember: Excellence develops in these areas when you...
1. Care about getting better.
2. Have a clear direction of what better looks like.
3. Get an education as to new ideas to pursue.
4. Embrace the discipline that will be needed.
5. Find a community of supporters who share your goals.

FRIENDSHIP

FITNESS

Date/Day:

YESTERDAY:

ASK BEAUTIFUL QUESTIONS:

BIBLE READ and NOTES:

TODAY'S SCHEDULE:

EAT THAT FROG:

MY DAILY HIGHLIGHT:

LEVEL 3 GRATITUDE:

AFFIRMATIONS ARE COOL:

Date/Day:

YESTERDAY:

ASK BEAUTIFUL QUESTIONS:

BIBLE READ and NOTES:

TODAY'S SCHEDULE:

EAT THAT FROG:

MY DAILY HIGHLIGHT:

LEVEL 3 GRATITUDE:

AFFIRMATIONS ARE COOL:

Date/Day:

YESTERDAY:

ASK BEAUTIFUL QUESTIONS:

BIBLE READ and NOTES:

TODAY'S SCHEDULE:

EAT THAT FROG:

MY DAILY HIGHLIGHT:

LEVEL 3 GRATITUDE:

AFFIRMATIONS ARE COOL:

Date/Day:

YESTERDAY:

ASK BEAUTIFUL QUESTIONS:

BIBLE READ and NOTES:

TODAY'S SCHEDULE:

EAT THAT FROG:

MY DAILY HIGHLIGHT:

LEVEL 3 GRATITUDE:

AFFIRMATIONS ARE COOL:

Date/Day:

YESTERDAY:

ASK BEAUTIFUL QUESTIONS:

BIBLE READ and NOTES:

TODAY'S SCHEDULE:

EAT THAT FROG:

MY DAILY HIGHLIGHT:

LEVEL 3 GRATITUDE:

AFFIRMATIONS ARE COOL:

Date/Day:

YESTERDAY:

ASK BEAUTIFUL QUESTIONS:

BIBLE READ and NOTES:

TODAY'S SCHEDULE:

EAT THAT FROG:

MY DAILY HIGHLIGHT:

LEVEL 3 GRATITUDE:

AFFIRMATIONS ARE COOL:

Date/Day:

YESTERDAY:

ASK BEAUTIFUL QUESTIONS:

BIBLE READ and NOTES:

TODAY'S SCHEDULE:

EAT THAT FROG:

MY DAILY HIGHLIGHT:

LEVEL 3 GRATITUDE:

AFFIRMATIONS ARE COOL:

4-FOLD EXCELLENCE

Weekly Progress

A great way to track progress is to excel in four key areas every week. If each week includes signs of measurable efforts in faith building, financial wisdom, friendship development, and fitness choices, this will add up to amazing progress! So as your week goes by, keep referencing back to this section to note specific things you did to grow in these areas.

FAITH

FINANCES

Remember: Excellence develops in these areas when you...
1. Care about getting better.
2. Have a clear direction of what better looks like.
3. Get an education as to new ideas to pursue.
4. Embrace the discipline that will be needed.
5. Find a community of supporters who share your goals.

FRIENDSHIP

FITNESS

Date/Day:

YESTERDAY:

ASK BEAUTIFUL QUESTIONS:

BIBLE READ and NOTES:

TODAY'S SCHEDULE:

EAT THAT FROG:

MY DAILY HIGHLIGHT:

LEVEL 3 GRATITUDE:

AFFIRMATIONS ARE COOL:

Date/Day:

YESTERDAY:

ASK BEAUTIFUL QUESTIONS:

BIBLE READ and NOTES:

TODAY'S SCHEDULE:

EAT THAT FROG:

MY DAILY HIGHLIGHT:

LEVEL 3 GRATITUDE:

AFFIRMATIONS ARE COOL:

Date/Day:

YESTERDAY:

ASK BEAUTIFUL QUESTIONS:

BIBLE READ and NOTES:

TODAY'S SCHEDULE:

EAT THAT FROG:

MY DAILY HIGHLIGHT:

LEVEL 3 GRATITUDE:

AFFIRMATIONS ARE COOL:

Date/Day:

YESTERDAY:

ASK BEAUTIFUL QUESTIONS:

BIBLE READ and NOTES:

TODAY'S SCHEDULE:

EAT THAT FROG:

MY DAILY HIGHLIGHT:

LEVEL 3 GRATITUDE:

AFFIRMATIONS ARE COOL:

Date/Day:

YESTERDAY:

ASK BEAUTIFUL QUESTIONS:

BIBLE READ and NOTES:

TODAY'S SCHEDULE:

EAT THAT FROG:

MY DAILY HIGHLIGHT:

LEVEL 3 GRATITUDE:

AFFIRMATIONS ARE COOL:

Date/Day:

YESTERDAY:

ASK BEAUTIFUL QUESTIONS:

BIBLE READ and NOTES:

TODAY'S SCHEDULE:

EAT THAT FROG:

MY DAILY HIGHLIGHT:

LEVEL 3 GRATITUDE:

AFFIRMATIONS ARE COOL:

Date/Day:

YESTERDAY:

ASK BEAUTIFUL QUESTIONS:

BIBLE READ and NOTES:

TODAY'S SCHEDULE:

EAT THAT FROG:

MY DAILY HIGHLIGHT:

LEVEL 3 GRATITUDE:

AFFIRMATIONS ARE COOL:

A great way to track progress is to excel in four key areas every week. If each week includes signs of measurable efforts in faith building, financial wisdom, friendship development, and fitness choices, this will add up to amazing progress! So as your week goes by, keep referencing back to this section to note specific things you did to grow in these areas.

FAITH

FINANCES

Remember: Excellence develops in these areas when you...
1. Care about getting better.
2. Have a clear direction of what better looks like.
3. Get an education as to new ideas to pursue.
4. Embrace the discipline that will be needed.
5. Find a community of supporters who share your goals.

FRIENDSHIP

FITNESS

Date/Day:

YESTERDAY:

ASK BEAUTIFUL QUESTIONS:

BIBLE READ and NOTES:

TODAY'S SCHEDULE:

EAT THAT FROG:

MY DAILY HIGHLIGHT:

LEVEL 3 GRATITUDE:

AFFIRMATIONS ARE COOL:

Date/Day:

YESTERDAY:

ASK BEAUTIFUL QUESTIONS:

BIBLE READ and NOTES:

TODAY'S SCHEDULE:

EAT THAT FROG:

MY DAILY HIGHLIGHT:

LEVEL 3 GRATITUDE:

AFFIRMATIONS ARE COOL:

Date/Day:

YESTERDAY:

ASK BEAUTIFUL QUESTIONS:

BIBLE READ and NOTES:

TODAY'S SCHEDULE:

EAT THAT FROG:

MY DAILY HIGHLIGHT:

LEVEL 3 GRATITUDE:

AFFIRMATIONS ARE COOL:

Date/Day:

YESTERDAY:

ASK BEAUTIFUL QUESTIONS:

BIBLE READ and NOTES:

TODAY'S SCHEDULE:

EAT THAT FROG:

MY DAILY HIGHLIGHT:

LEVEL 3 GRATITUDE:

AFFIRMATIONS ARE COOL:

Date/Day:

YESTERDAY:

ASK BEAUTIFUL QUESTIONS:

BIBLE READ and NOTES:

TODAY'S SCHEDULE:

EAT THAT FROG:

MY DAILY HIGHLIGHT:

LEVEL 3 GRATITUDE:

AFFIRMATIONS ARE COOL:

Date/Day:

YESTERDAY:

ASK BEAUTIFUL QUESTIONS:

BIBLE READ and NOTES:

TODAY'S SCHEDULE:

EAT THAT FROG:

MY DAILY HIGHLIGHT:

LEVEL 3 GRATITUDE:

AFFIRMATIONS ARE COOL:

Date/Day:

YESTERDAY:

ASK BEAUTIFUL QUESTIONS:

BIBLE READ and NOTES:

TODAY'S SCHEDULE:

EAT THAT FROG:

MY DAILY HIGHLIGHT:

LEVEL 3 GRATITUDE:

AFFIRMATIONS ARE COOL:

Printed in the USA
CPSIA information can be obtained
at www.ICGtesting.com
LVHW071723291124
797893LV00015B/387
9781964805078